DAILY
MEDICINE

WAYNE WILLIAM SNELLGROVE

DEDICATION

This book is dedicated to life, the perpetuation and the celebration of all life.

All meditations have been guided to me from the Spirit, the source of all love and light.

A special dedication to my teachers, all of them, especially those who have guided me in my own personal healing and shown me how to love again, that I can always act in love, for love, and with love. Reminding me that I am a true source of great, wonderful, and powerful love and light.

Thank you Grandfather Tony Stonehawk, Thomas Keenewall, and fathers Robert Kayseas and Richard Snellgrove. And of course, my wife and first editor, Charlotte Miller-Snellgrove.

This book would not possible if it weren't for the love and support from my wife Charlotte.

I love you all.

INTRODUCTION

THERE IS SPIRITUAL POETRY everywhere. Spiritual lessons are everywhere; this is what the Spirit has told me. This book is dedicated to those teachings.

This book has evolved from sharing simple truths from the Spirit on my social media pages for my own spiritual recovery. At first, it was others peoples' messages, and slowly, over time, it would include a few of mine. The big change happened when I created and started my own prayer. "Creator, I will go wherever you want me to go, and do whatever you what me to do." This prayer is in the true spirit of the "hollow bone" indigenous spiritual analogy for conduit for the Spirit, allowing the Spirit to flow through me.

My indigenous father, Robert Kayseas, and I spoke at length before he died about the lost ceremony of listening. It is one of the many languages of the Spirit but the first one we have to learn before we speak.

Since then, I have taken this medicine of listening to deep and wonderful levels in my life, beginning with quieting my mind and listening for the sound of my own heartbeat.

As I continued, the things I listened to began to speak in silent whispers and echoing ancestral voices. I realized all our ancestors, the trees, the winged, the insects, the four-leggeds, the fish people, all nations, all life had a voice, had a song, and had wisdom for us. All life had something to offer humanity.

This book is what they have said.

SUGGESTED INSTRUCTIONS

This book, "Daily Medicine," is a Spiritual Prayer book, meant to be read and then prayed with each individual guided meditation. Each Meditation is directly from Spirit and is designed to enhance your personal understanding of the Spirit.

With each quote, the suggestion is to sit with it, not just gloss over the words quickly as a rote routine. As our understanding of the Spirit grows, so will our understanding of these quotes. What we read and understand today may have an entirely different meaning within a month or over the next couple of years. The idea is to stay in prayer and journey with these meditations.

The Medicine Wheel talks about walking our personal spiritual path which we Indigenous call the Red Road. We travel from innocence to wisdom. We are all walking this path whether we embrace this concept or understand it. Some of us are a little further along in our understanding of indigenous spiritual wisdom, some are not yet that far along. Wherever you are is okay. None are meant to be judged. We are all here to help each other along this

Spiritual path.

The terms God, Creator, and Great Spirit are used interchangeably. None have any denominational interpretation. All are spiritual names for the Great source, the divine being.

JANUARY

I

JANUARY

If you want your old life to end, let it end with your last breath. If you want a new life, let it begin with your next breath.

2

JANUARY

The sunrise does not define itself by last night's darkness.

———◈———

3

JANUARY

When we make a declaration to the world that we are going to have a beautiful life despite all our mistakes and misfortune, we have come into our power.

———◆———

4

JANUARY

Air is life. Earth is life. Fire is life. Water is life. Trees are life. Animals are life. Breath is life. Prayer is life. The ceremony is life.

———◈———

5

JANUARY

Flowers do not worry if they are going to bloom.

———◈———

6

JANUARY

The Spirits' answer to the lonely is that they are never alone.

———◆———

7

JANUARY

The lessons of the darkness are to walk through it.
The lessons of the light are to become it.

———◈———

8

JANUARY

Humanity has never been more brilliant than when it remembers its own humanity.

———◈———

9

JANUARY

Mother Earth is craving an intimate and prayerful
relationship with you.

———◈———

10

JANUARY

The original sound healing is talking kindly to each other.

———◆———

II

JANUARY

We must look at Mother Earth not as a resource for some,
but as a responsibility for all.

———◆———

12

JANUARY

Our ancestors told us: not all languages are spoken,
and not all voices can be heard. But we can still
communicate with all.

13

JANUARY

Your diploma doesn't define your intelligence.
Your religion doesn't define your spirituality.
Your past doesn't define you as a person.

———◆———

14

JANUARY

Mother Earth has no interest in seeing us become rich,
but she gives us everything to become wealthy.

———◈———

15

JANUARY

The dream of the wind is to blow. The dream of the sun is to shine. The dream of the rain is to fall. The dream of our ancestors to be remembered.

———◆———

16

JANUARY

Fear not the challenges of darkness. Fear only that you won't allow love and light to enter your heart.

———◈———

17

JANUARY

Look into my eyes and you will see me. Listen to my voice
and you will hear me. Walk with me and you will grow
with me. Listen to my heart and you will understand me.

18

JANUARY

Kindness is gentleness, Gentleness is compassion.
Compassion is love.
Unfortunately, humanity is always looking for a guru,
teacher, or master, someone who supposedly has become
one with everything. Because of our humanity, many
teachers and gurus fall short, and we become disillusioned.
If you are looking for a guru or master, let it begin with
Mother Earth. We can begin by simply welcoming the new
dawn in a beautiful way.

———◆———

19

JANUARY

Connecting to Mother Earth is an antidepressant.
Hugging a tree is an antidepressant.
Admiring a beautiful flower is an antidepressant.
Watching the sunrise is an antidepressant.
Bare-footing on Mother Earth an antidepressant.
Loving Mother Earth is an antidepressant.

———◈———

20

JANUARY

Every time a flower blooms, a relative returns.
Every time bird hatches, a relative returns.
Every time a wolf pup is born, a relative returns.
Every time it rains, a relative returns.
Every time the sun comes up, a relative returns.

———◈———

21

JANUARY

Those who have mastered the truth began
with seeing their own.

———◈———

22

JANUARY

Part of understanding love is acknowledging diversity and
the power of Unity.
Love is not love when we divide and create separation.

———◆———

23

JANUARY

If we want our lives to matter and have meaning, we must begin by telling and showing others that their lives matter and have meaning.

———◆———

24

JANUARY

Our prayers begin our spiritual roots,
grounding us to the collective strength of both
the seen and the unseen worlds.

———◈———

25

JANUARY

You deserve the gift of giving love.

———◈———

26

JANUARY

The greatest threat to humanity is man's indifference to it.

———◆———

27

JANUARY

Where there is light there is always prayer. Where there is prayer there is always compassion. Where there is compassion there is always love. Where there is love there is always life. Where there is life there is always light.

———◆———

28

JANUARY

Be thankful for your last breath and hopeful for your next because both are a gift.

———◈———

29

JANUARY

Gratitude remembers what sadness, resentment
and loneliness cannot.

30

JANUARY

Let your love from the last moment pollinate your next.

———◈———

31

JANUARY

Our Spiritual path: I can, I will, I do.

———◈———

FEBRUARY

I

FEBRUARY

The most important moment of our lives is truly learning to live in this one.

————◆————

2

FEBRUARY

The simple paradox in our lives is that we must face
our fears to live in peace.

———◆———

3

FEBRUARY

If we can't reach our own sacred center,
it will be hard for us to find, hear, or see anyone else's.

———◈———

4
FEBRUARY

Often the most broken among us become
the most beautiful.

———◆———

5

FEBRUARY

Healing is a sacred place where everyone belongs.

———◆———

6

FEBRUARY

Our spiritual journey consists of traveling inward to our
vast and beautiful realms of inner oceans, high and mighty
mountains to find that place of peace
amid the storms of life.

———◆———

7

FEBRUARY

The medicine wheel teaches us, it is the beauty within ourselves that enables us to see the beauty in the wounded.

———◈———

8

FEBRUARY

Our spiritual choice is either listen to the noise
or dance to the music.

———◈———

9

FEBRUARY

The deepest, darkest places in our hearts are not sources
of weakness.
They are sources of untapped strength and courage.

———◈———

IO

FEBRUARY

Some lessons can only be learned before the storm.
Some lessons can only be learned in the storm.
Some lessons can only be learned after the storm.

———◈———

II

FEBRUARY

Sometimes we have to remind ourselves
to just love ourselves.

———◆———

I2

FEBRUARY

When it comes from our heart,
it can't help but touch someone else's.

———◈———

13

FEBRUARY

Mother Earth has a heritage and culture
unto herself that humanity knows little of.

———◆———

14

FEBRUARY

If there is a place inside us for prayer, there is a place inside us for growth. If there is a place inside for growth, there is a place inside for healing. If there is a place inside us for healing, there is a place for love.

———◈———

15

FEBRUARY

Sometimes we confuse those events that we think will
hurt us with those events that will heal us
and guide us home.

———◆———

16

FEBRUARY

The essence of life is that we are connected to everything.
The essence of love is that everything is connected to us.

———◈———

17

FEBRUARY

There are always messages available to us from the Spirit. They are found in every situation and at any time. We must continually be aware and available. Some are found in silence. Others are found within the noise and haste. Still others are found in darkness.

———◈———

18

FEBRUARY

The prayers of Mother Earth flow within each of us,
constantly moving with us and for us.

19

FEBRUARY

Medicine Wheel teaching:
Every sunset has a sunrise. Every sunrise has a sunset.

20

FEBRUARY

The paradox of living a spiritual life is that
the smaller the miracle we see,
the more love we carry.

———◆———

21

FEBRUARY

The essence of love dwells when you walk with me
and I walk with you.

❖

22

FEBRUARY

Ascending into our humanness
is ascending into love.

———◆———

23

FEBRUARY

True spiritual warriors won't show their greatness.
Their greatness is found by leading you to yours.

———◈———

24

FEBRUARY

Sometimes true courage is just finding a way
to allow yourself to be loved.

———◆———

25

FEBRUARY

Trying to find a blessing in life and not finding one
is like looking for air and not finding any.

———◈———

26

FEBRUARY

Humility is the machine that drives spiritual growth.

———◆———

27

FEBRUARY

We are only here on Earth because of prayers made on behalf of our ancestors. They prayed for life. To come full circle and continue living in that sacred flow, we must offer those prayers up for future generations.

———◆———

28

FEBRUARY

It is in the presence of our own humility
that we are able usher in miracles.

———◆———

29

FEBRUARY

Reconciliation between nations won't work until we have begun reconciliation between man and Mother Earth.

———◈———

MARCH

I

MARCH

I am the sacred light that shines above me. I am the sacred water that flows through me. I am the sacred wind that blows around me. I am the sacred fire that burns within me. I am the sacred Earth that encompasses me.

———◆———

2

MARCH

This world would be a better place if we learned to leave prayers wherever we went instead of leaving opinions.

———◆———

3
MARCH

We share common destiny with our prayers.

4

MARCH

Our voice and our thoughts are endless prayers
living in an endless ceremony.

———◆———

5

MARCH

We are always a reflection of the light that we give.

———◆———

6

MARCH

The wounds that are never healed are the ones that are never acknowledged.

———◆———

7

MARCH

The deeper the wound, the deeper the wisdom.

———◆———

8

MARCH

I am only as powerful as my last prayer
and as hopeful as my next.

———◆———

9

MARCH

Change your prayer, changes your attitude.
Change your attitude, changes your walk.
Change your walk, changes your world.

———◈———

IO

MARCH

What defines us as a species is how we treat our women,
up to and including our Mother Earth.
This, above all else, will decide our fate.
Why do we continue to kill, diminish, separate ourselves
from the very divine feminine who gave us life
in the first place?

———◆———

II

MARCH

There is always a better life
on the other side of gratitude.

———◆———

12

MARCH

We never really know anyone until we pray with them.
We never really know ourselves until we pray for them.

———◆———

13

MARCH

Let us always meet our Creator at sunrise with prayer and offerings of thanks. As we do, in silence ask what the Great Spirit may need from us. Make clear we are ready, willing, and able to do our part to help Creator. This makes good relations with Creator.

Only after expressing and offering gratitude can we ask about what we need. We tell Creator our dreams, wishes, and aspirations. To come full circle, we must learn to carry all these prayers with us during the day.

14

MARCH

The miracle of Mother Earth is no matter how wounded,
no matter how much we destroy her,
she never stops growing.

———◈———

15

MARCH

The love you give is the love you carry,
the hurt you give is the hurt you carry.

———◈———

16

MARCH

People walking without the guidance of those who have
come before us is like birds trying to fly without wings. It
is in the teachings of our elders that we learn how to walk.
It is in the teachings of our ancestors that
we learn how to fly.

———◈———

17

MARCH

One of the basic teachings of the medicine wheel is that spiritual realms are reflected in the physical world. The wind blows from every direction, so must wisdom come from every direction.

———◈———

18

MARCH

Our ancestors left us footprints to follow, but they were wise because we can only can see them with our hearts.

———◈———

19

MARCH

Whenever love is shared anywhere,
it helps restore balance everywhere.

———◈———

20

MARCH

The sunrise is one of our closest relatives.
We should always greet it as gently as a newborn baby.
We must carry that gentleness with us to all
our relatives.

———◈———

21

MARCH

There isn't a gender hierarchy when it comes to the Great Spirit. The Great Spirit is a perfect and pure representation of both divine feminine and masculine.

———⋘◇⋙———

22

MARCH

Nothing is more horrific than competing with our own fears, because we always lose.

———◈———

23

MARCH

Let us remember Mother Earth is our
ultimate feminine warrior.

———◆———

24

MARCH

Don't make love your destination.
Let love be your "right here, right now,"
and you have reached your destination.

———◈———

25

MARCH

Saying "thank you" is never a wasted prayer.

———◆———

26

MARCH

Like raindrops on a pond rippling out,
our prayers and acts of kindness ripple directly
to the center of the universe.

———◈———

27

MARCH

Prayer is a sacred ceremony.

———◈———

28

MARCH

We should learn to master our listening
before we master giving our opinions.

29

MARCH

The brilliance of the butterfly is when it
remembers it was a caterpillar.

———◆———

30

MARCH

God is love. And any love that we give is much more God's success than ours, because we are only a conduit, a hollow bone for his love.

31

MARCH

The birth of sadness is often the lack of gratitude.

———◆———

APRIL

I

APRIL

Mother Earth has memories of what it is like to be loved,
honored and remembered. As a species it is up to us to
pray and listen until we can hear her memories
of love and honor.

———◈———

2

APRIL

The wisdom of listening is often forgotten when we speak.

———◆———

3

APRIL

We must listen to the stories of those who came before us
so we can carry those stories to future generations.

———◈———

4
APRIL

If you're not loving yourself, the thing you are
fighting is often only you.

———◈———

5
APRIL

Inside every one of us is a flower that wants to bloom, a sun that wants to rise, and a song that wants to be sung.

———◈———

6

APRIL

The rain inside looks like tears. They are needed to help us heal, and help us feel. The tears cleanse our spirits and water our spiritual garden.

———◈———

7
APRIL

The peaceful are peaceful because they continually
practice peaceful ways and peaceful prayers.

———◆———

8

APRIL

Silence is a gift of wisdom often used by those who have learned that listening is more powerful than speaking.

———◈———

9
APRIL

In each one of us lies a beautiful promise of a new spring.

IO

APRIL

The poetry of Mother Earth is found in all living things.
It is written in the colors she wears and
the music she sings.

———◆———

II

APRIL

There is nothing confusing about the truth
unless you're trying to hide from it.

———◆———

12

APRIL

The worst sound of injustice sounds like
silence from the masses.

———◈———

13

APRIL

Sometimes our greatest mistake is
not looking at our last one.

———◆———

14
APRIL

The dream of happiness is to share it.

———◈———

15

APRIL

Love gives us back the life that fear took away.

———◆———

16

APRIL

Every day is a privilege, not a right.

———◈———

17

APRIL

The medicine of the river is patience; it is able to move mountains. It just takes time.

———◆———

18

APRIL

When our sacred women begin to heal, they will begin to
speak, and when they speak, humanity will begin to heal,
and when humanity begins to heal,
the Earth will begin to heal.

———◈———

19

APRIL

The spiritual life of a prayer has four parts:
1. Listen. 2. Pray. 3. Action. 4. Repeat.

———◆———

20

APRIL

Like a spiraling circle toward the center,
loving all creation will bring us closer to our Creator.

———◆———

21

APRIL

We must listen to the voice of the caterpillar as much as we listen to the voice of the cocoon. We must listen to the voice of the cocoon as much as we listen to the butterfly. They are all connected.

22

APRIL

The absence of God is only an illusion.

———◈———

23

APRIL

Humanity's worst enemy isn't hate or even fear.
It is apathy.

———◈———

24

APRIL

Finding heaven is allowing love to enter our hearts.

———◈———

25

APRIL

There is always beauty in those things once broken.

———◈———

26

APRIL

In Creator's economy nothing is wasted; even in our most difficult and darkest challenges lies a beautiful opportunity for growth and a better life.

———◆———

27

APRIL

The forgotten sacred gifts that the Great Spirit gave humanity was the opportunity and capability of not only speaking for all life, but protecting all life.

———◈———

28

APRIL

Love isn't that thing we keep. Our journey is to accept it, become it, then give it away. Only after giving it away is our love renewed. This is the flow we must live in.

———◈———

29

APRIL

The biggest threat to Mother Earth is believing
someone else will save her.

———◈———

30
APRIL

One of the greatest gifts we can give to our
own healing is vulnerability.

———◆———

MAY

I

MAY

Maybe the morning birds
are singing just for you.

———◈———

2

MAY

Real courage is bringing death to those things
within us that no longer serve life.

———◆———

3

MAY

The Medicine Wheel teaches us to be gentle with ourselves as we transition from one season of our lives to the next. Like summer into fall. Winter into spring.

———◆———

4
MAY

Selfishness is an inward facing spiritual disease
that robs us of our ability to learn, grow,
see, feel and listen.

———◈———

5

MAY

An often overlooked and under-appreciated
spiritual experience is waking up.

———◈———

6

MAY

The ancient ones say there is no separation between
prayer and talking, prayer and thoughts.
Let every word and thought be prayerful.

———◆———

7

MAY

Our untold, and therefore unhealed, stories are
often the root of all our self-deception.

———◆———

8

MAY

What may seem foolish to the heart
may be exactly what the heart needs to heal.

———◈———

9

MAY

Walking through fear has always been the path.

———◆———

IO

MAY

If you want to help save Mother Earth, plant a tree, and as you water it every day, tell it you love it.

———◈———

II

MAY

The Spiritual paradox is the more love we carry
the lighter the load.

———◆———

12

MAY

We are created by love, to love, and to remember
we are love.

———◆———

13

MAY

Let us not forget that our spiritual teachers
are still human.

———◈———

14

MAY

The tapestry of our lives is not only woven
in our prayers but by the way we walk with them.

———◈———

15

MAY

There is no material solution to a spiritual problem.
There is no sexual solution to a spiritual problem.
There is no chemical solution to a spiritual problem.
The only solution to a spiritual problem is spiritual.

———◆———

16

MAY

Offering love is a skill no one can take away from you.

———◆———

17

MAY

Our only block to compassion is our own refusal.

———◈———

18

MAY

We never want to feign forgiveness; it is an ongoing
process that we can start or continue at any time.

———◇———

19

MAY

We do not create beauty by just praying about it.
We create beauty by living it.
We do not create peace by just praying about it.
We create peace by living it.

———◈———

20

MAY

Everything before the truth is an illusion.

———◈———

21

MAY

Mother Earth is a beautiful picture of
what humanity should look like.

———◈———

22

MAY

The first miracle of the day is life. The last miracle of the day is life. Everything in between should be focused on honoring, loving and nurturing that life.

———◆———

23

MAY

If you woke up today there is a beautiful,
divine source that believes in you.

———◆———

24

MAY

It is wonderful to acknowledge the beauty of the sunrise.
It is quite another to carry that beauty
with you wherever you go.

———◈———

25

MAY

It is spiritual to to be kind. It is spiritual to be compassionate. It is spiritual to forgive. It is spiritual to heal. It is spiritual to feel fear. It is spiritual to be sad. It is spiritual to cry. It is spiritual to feel anger. It is spiritual to be imperfect. All these characteristics and feelings simply mean it is spiritual to be human.

———◆———

26

MAY

Our prayers determine our future. We must choose our
words wisely. For every thought is not only a prayer but a
creation of things to come.

———◆———

27

MAY

Our spiritual journey brings us to what we were, to who we want to to be. The path to get there is filled with fears we have to walk through. The truth is our guide. The path is lighted by those who have walked the road before us: our ancestors.

———◈———

28

MAY

Our gift to the world is found
in the love that we share.

———◆———

29

MAY

Every truth we share makes it that much easier
to share the next truth. Every lie we tell makes it that
much easier to tell the next lie.

———◈———

30

MAY

Don't let your next mistake be not
forgiving others of their last.

———◆———

31

MAY

When you decide to love
nothing will stop you;
until then almost everything will.

———◈———

JUNE

I

JUNE

The best revenge is forgiveness.

———◆———

2

JUNE

Creating a beautiful, personal relationship
with Mother Earth is one of humanity's
most forgotten ceremonies.

———◆———

3

JUNE

When we shift our perception of what God
is doing to us to what God is doing for us,
our lives will never be the same.

———◆———

4
JUNE

Worrying doesn't replace
anything but faith.

———◆———

5
JUNE

Humility is the beginning of abundance.

———◈———

6

JUNE

The outcome of hate is being more hateful.
The outcome of love is being more loving.

———◆———

7

JUNE

To keep the enthusiasm high, always act as if you are seeing something for the first time; if you have trouble with that, act as if you are seeing it for the last time.

———◈———

8

JUNE

The spiritually foolish sleep in environments
that keep them asleep.
The spiritually awake sleep in environments
that keep them awake.

———◆———

9

JUNE

The best result worrying ever got
was more worrying.

———◆———

10

JUNE

In Mother Nature, so much love is packed into small things. So small we often overlook them. Every pine needle, every drop of dew, every snowflake, every leaf, every sunset and sunrise.

———◆———

II

JUNE

We don't really understand the power of our prayers until we walk with them. We must learn to hold on to them from sunrise to sunset, month to month, season to season. Only then do we realize their power.

———◈———

12

JUNE

Remember our own voice is a sacred wind.
Treat it as such.

———◈———

13

JUNE

Those poor in Spirit will take offense and assign blame.
Those strong in Spirit will take the lesson and forgive.

———◆———

14

JUNE

It is in the realm of controversy over heaven
that we miss heaven completely.

———◆———

15

JUNE

Not dealing with being uncomfortable only
makes us that much more uncomfortable.

———◆———

16

JUNE

Fear feeds the unawakened.
Faith feeds the unshakable.

———◆———

17

JUNE

The loud show us how weak they are.
The gentle show us how strong they are.

———◆———

18

JUNE

Our destiny should always include helping others.
If it does not, we are heading toward
the wrong destination.

———◈———

19

JUNE

Our sacred breath carries our sacred prayers
to a sacred place.

20

JUNE

How we talk to the animals is how we talk to ourselves.
How we listen to the trees is how we listen to ourselves.
How we treat Mother Earth is how we treat ourselves.

———◆———

21

JUNE

Our job is to leave this world a little better place
than before we arrived. We do this not only for us
but for our future seven generations.

———◆———

22

JUNE

Worrying is going back to tomorrow's results.

———◆———

23

JUNE

Love is courage.
Love is patience.
Love is listening.
Love is the wind.
Love is the incoming tide.
Love is the rainstorm.
Love is the sunset.
Love is the morning birds singing.
Love is the change of the seasons.
Love is everywhere all the time.

———◈———

24

JUNE

A day that begins without prayer is a day
that begins without direction.

———◈———

25

JUNE

Love is the sacred perfume of the Spirit.

———◈———

26

JUNE

Our darkness is just as sacred
as our light.

———◈———

27

JUNE

Two things can give life to itself:.
Love and hate.
It is up to you which life you choose.

———◆———

28

JUNE

When we work with God, for God, and next to God,
we realize all miracles are from God.

—◈—

29

JUNE

People often miss the beautiful colors of the clouds
because they fear the storm.

———◆———

30

JUNE

Hope is the beam of light we send out to the universe.
Our attitude decides how bright it is.
Our determination decides how far it goes.

———◈———

JULY

I

JULY

The purpose of life is to celebrate it.

—◆—

2

JULY

If we are not humbled by the mere fact that
we woke up this morning, then we are forgetting the
greatest gift ever given to us.

———◈———

3
JULY

The first test of love is humility,
the last test of love is humility,
the only test of love is humility.

———◆———

4

JULY

Within our hearts is the sacred flame
of a thousand fires, a beautiful gift
given to us by our ancestors.

———◆———

5

JULY

Let faith be your guide.
Let prayer be your voice.
Let courage be your strength.
Let love be your vision.

—◆—

6

JULY

May your days be filled with prayers.
May your prayers be filled with healing.
May your healing be filled with love.
May your love create your life.
May your life be filled with ceremony.
May your ceremony be the message
for the entire world to see.

———◈———

7

JULY

The medicine of the sunrise is not only to let it
touch your skin, but let it enter your heart.
The medicine of the heart is not to keep it,
but to share it.

———◈———

8

JULY

Our elders are a window into our ancestral wisdom.
That wisdom will help guide us into the future.

———◆———

9

JULY

Love is the original ceremony.

———◆———

10

JULY

The definition of perfection is trying.

———◈———

II

JULY

The mountain grows according to our fears.

———◆———

12

JULY

Pray hard, then listen until you hear the voice of the trees;
listen until you hear the whispers of the wandering winds;
listen until you hear the songs of the misty mountains;
listen until you hear the ballads of the running water;
listen until you hear the languages of the animals. Only
then will you hear the true sounds of your own voice and
understand their voices are yours.

———◈———

13

JULY

Our spiritual growth is as painful as our resistance to it.

———◈———

14
JULY

Transparency is the color of humility.

———◆———

15

JULY

Praying without listening is like
breathing in without breathing out.

———◆———

16

JULY

If I listen; I hear. If I hear; I do. If I do; I learn.
If I learn; I grow.

———◈———

17

JULY

The medicine wheel doesn't say one part of life or season
is any harder, easier or better than another.
All it says is let it flow in and through like
the seasons, the rivers, and the wind.

———◈———

18

JULY

If there is any magic to be found, it is in the truth.

———◆———

19

JULY

The mountains are my muscles.
The trees are my arms.
The air is my breath.
The river is my blood.
The wind is my songs.
The oceans are my dreams.

———◈———

20

JULY

Mother Earth is a living, breathing organism.
She has emotions and feelings just like another creature.
She feels pain, has memories and dreams. She longs to be
loved and remembered, honored, treated with beauty.

———◈———

21

JULY

Often God's guidance and strength look like
perseverance and patience.

———◈———

22

JULY

Humanity's spiritual dyslexia:
speaking rather than listening.
We must learn to let listening be our first
form of communication and speaking our last.

———◈———

23

JULY

There is only one language that can heal
spiritual diseases: the truth.

———◈———

24

JULY

The next flower that blooms may be you;
don't give up.

———◆———

25

JULY

Leadership is not about politics or power.
It is about providing a space for the people
to find their personal power and heal.

———◆———

26

JULY

Build a deep relationship with your ancestors
and you will find your path.
Build a deep relationship with Mother Earth
and you will find yourself.

———◈———

27

JULY

If we are not appreciating and building a wonderful relationship with Mother Earth and all her life, then we are missing out on the most beautiful part of ours.

———◈———

28

JULY

The story of the seed:
The baby seed knew the journey in front of her. After
being born, dropped in the dirt, surrounded by darkness,
she knew her only chance of survival was to grow in the
dark until she reached the light.
And after, she knew then that was only the beginning.

———◆———

29

JULY

Our Indigenous spiritual path is the Red Road.
It is a road not seen in any direction but a conscious
connection to all roads, all directions and to all life.

———◆———

30

JULY

Let us always be grateful...
nights turn into day,
winters into spring,
summers into fall,
rains into life,
wounds into wisdom,
prayers into patience.

31

JULY

The sunrise doesn't end until it sets.

———◈———

AUGUST

I

AUGUST

When a flower dies here,
it blooms in the next world.

———◈———

2

AUGUST

We have a common destiny with the trees.
We have a common destiny with the air.
We have a common destiny with the water.
We have a common destiny with the animals.
We have common destiny with the mountains.
We have a common destiny with the seasons.
We have a common destiny with Mother Earth.

———◈———

3

AUGUST

Unity should be humanity's religion.

4
AUGUST

Racism is a clear sign of
humanity's spiritual infancy.

———◆———

5

AUGUST

Air is the color of humility.
Water is the color of life.
Fire is the color of the flame within.
Earth is the color of the Spirit.

———◈———

6

AUGUST

When an Indigenous Grandmother starts singing,
she begins to heal herself.
When the Grandmothers start singing together,
the world begins to heal.

———◆———

7

AUGUST

Those spiritual lessons we try to hide from
always get in our way.

———◈———

8

AUGUST

Eagles never worry about what pigeons say.

———◈———

9

AUGUST

A strong woman stands up for herself.
A stronger woman stands up for other women.
The strongest woman stands up for Mother Earth.

———◆———

10

AUGUST

Flower medicine:
Flowers do not begin to bloom from the outside in,
they bloom from the inside out.

———◆———

II

AUGUST

To embrace the balance we want to live in,
we must first embrace the unbalance.
To embrace healing, we must embrace
what is unhealed.

———◈———

12

AUGUST

Let gratitude be the beginning of everything.

———◆———

13

AUGUST

There is an entire life in every prayer.
And in every life is an entire prayer.

———◆———

14

AUGUST

Humanity's greatest and hardest mystery is
figuring out we are all brothers and sisters.

———◈———

15

AUGUST

Our world is reduced, our vision blurred and the
flow of life fades into stillness when we don't add
Creator into everything we do.

———◆———

16

AUGUST

The original sound healing is listening to
the music of Mother Earth.

———◆———

17

AUGUST

Our gratitude will always be incomplete
until we help someone else.

———◈———

18

AUGUST

We must learn to see far beyond what our empathy can see for humanity to survive.

———◆———

19

AUGUST

Every part of Mother Earth, every tree, every stone,
leaf, dust, plant, has a story that needs to be heard.
They are family. They have a story and a healing for
all of us. These are lessons from the past to
guide us to a better future.

———◆———

20

AUGUST

If the land is sick, we will become sick.
If we are sick, our children will be sick.
If they are sick, the next generations will be sick.

———◈———

21

AUGUST

Hold one hand toward the sky and one hand on the ground until you realize you are a relative of both.

———◈———

22

AUGUST

Patience is the flower waiting for the storm.
Perseverance is the flower enduring the storm.
Maturity is the flower growing from the storm.

———◆———

23

AUGUST

Everything you see with your eyes
is the same thing that is within you.
When you look over the deep night sky,
that is the same sky within you.
When you look over the vast oceans,
those are the same oceans within you.
When you look at a drop of morning dew,
that is the same drop within you.
When you look over the cold winters,
that is the same winter within you.
When you look over the new spring,
that is the same new spring within you.
When you look over the summer rains,
that is the same summer rain within you.

———◆———

24

AUGUST

The truth is like the weather; the less truth we speak,
the darker the clouds and the harder it is to see.
Pure truth is like a sunny day; it travels far
and can be seen by many.

———◈———

25

AUGUST

Humility doesn't lead us to the truth, it is the truth.

———◈———

26

AUGUST

The Medicine Wheel teaches us there is a time for sadness
when the birds take their songs south for the winter.
But then it also teaches us happiness, too,
when the birds come back for the spring.

———◈———

27

AUGUST

Hope whispers to your dreams.
Your dreams whisper to your prayers.
Your prayers are a whisper to God.
God whispers to your life.

———◆———

28

AUGUST

We should ask ourselves:
do my thoughts, prayers and actions support
the person I want to be
and the life I want to live?

———◆———

29

AUGUST

Let my prayers burn brighter than the
fires of life that burn around me.
Let my prayers flow stronger than the storms around me.
Let my prayers blow stronger than the winds around me.

———◆———

30

AUGUST

Within every seed, a beautiful flower resides.
Within every prayer, a beautiful life resides.

———◆———

31

AUGUST

As indigenous, our moral compass is based
on our relationship with Mother Earth.
As a species, this helps restore balance
back into our unbalanced humanity.

———◆———

SEPTEMBER

I

SEPTEMBER

The definition of healer and lover are
the same. We want everything for you
but nothing from you.

———◆———

2

SEPTEMBER

If our personal growth and transformation
do not include the protection and healing
of Mother Earth, it is incomplete.

———◆———

3

SEPTEMBER

Insanity is serving a master that doesn't serve you,
like hate, greed, resentment, and fear.

———◈———

4

SEPTEMBER

One of our most forgotten ceremonies
is honoring our sacred women.

———◈———

5

SEPTEMBER

Our job as healers is not to awaken the sleeping
but to create a safe space for them
to wake up on their own.

———◆———

6

SEPTEMBER

Money shouldn't bring privilege,
only responsibility.

———◆———

7

SEPTEMBER

We must learn to base our opinions on prayers.

———◆———

8

SEPTEMBER

Our book of memories begins
with our ancestors.

———◈———

9

SEPTEMBER

Worrying is carrying around wounds
we don't have.

10

SEPTEMBER

I am my surroundings. And my surroundings are me.
I am Mother Earth. And Mother Earth is me.
I am the sunrise. And the sunrise is me.
I am the flowing water. And the flowing water is me.
I am the fire. And the fire is me.
I am the wind. And the wind is me.
I am the trees. And the trees are me.
I am the summer. And the summer is me.
I am the winter. And the winter is me.
I am the rain. And the rain is me.
I am the blooming flower. And the blooming flower is me.
I am my surroundings. And my surroundings are me.

———◈———

II

SEPTEMBER

Our spiritual healing is only as equal as our honesty.

———◆———

12

SEPTEMBER

Mother Earth needs three things from us:
to listen to her, to love her, and to protect her.

———◆———

13

SEPTEMBER

People say respect is earned. I disagree.
Respect is always given; not because people deserve it,
but because it is a clear and powerful
statement of my character.

———◆———

14

SEPTEMBER

People are often lonely because they fail to create a
healthy relationship with those beautiful and
powerful spirits around them, like the trees, the winds,
the sun and especially Mother Earth.

———◈———

15

SEPTEMBER

There are many forms of spiritual disease.
The worst is pretending to be healthy or happy
when you are not.

———◈———

16

SEPTEMBER

Medicine Wheel teachings:
The medicine wheel teaches us we are all walking a path
from spiritual innocence to wisdom whether we like it
or understand it. This is our life's journey.
We cannot stop or delay this process.
It is ongoing from birth to death.
The most important part of our journey
is respecting others on theirs.

———◆———

17

SEPTEMBER

Truth is the language the Spirit always understands.

———◈———

18

SEPTEMBER

The spiritual principle behind abundance is giving.

———◆———

19

SEPTEMBER

Often we have to walk through our own insanity
to find our sanity.

———◆———

20

SEPTEMBER

The Great Spirit resides in all living things.
Therefore, all living things are sacred.
There is no hierarchy of the sacred.
We are all equal.

———◆———

21

SEPTEMBER

Humanity's greatest adventure is not
finding life on other planets, but
finding it within one's self.

———◈———

22

SEPTEMBER

The awakened mind doesn't tell others it's awake.
Those who do, aren't awakened.
They are still asleep.

———◈———

23

SEPTEMBER

Some days we are guided by a thousand points of light.
Other days we are only guided by the light
we have shared with others.

———◆———

24

SEPTEMBER

We have to remember there is a place for healing for everyone, whether it is individually, in groups or community. All have a place in the sacred circle.

———◆———

25

SEPTEMBER

It is time humanity realizes we are people of Earth; one race, one heart, one mind, one people.

———◆———

26

SEPTEMBER

If we argue with people's shortcomings and weaknesses,
it doesn't reveal their character defects.
It reveals our own.

———◆———

27

SEPTEMBER

The thunder is always calling us.
The rain is always calling us.
The sun is always calling us.
The moon is always calling us.
The seasons are always calling us.
They all have stories and lessons for us.

———◆———

28

SEPTEMBER

Every day a little part of us dies.
Every day another part is reborn.
It is up to us to decide which parts.

———◆———

29

SEPTEMBER

A loving mind will think in loving ways.
An unhealed mind will think in unhealed ways.
A wounded mind will think in wounded ways.
A healed mind will think in healed ways.

30
SEPTEMBER

We must remember:
people will treat us where they are,
not where we are.
We do our best not to take it personally.

———◈———

OCTOBER

I

OCTOBER

Every part of Mother Earth has a song.
The water, the trees, the wind, the fire, the stones
and each animal. It is important to listen
to their medicine songs.
It creates a bond, an instant connection.

———◆———

2

OCTOBER

We must get away from speaking ill of the darkness
and fear we have to walk through.
Let us simply accept these as part of our healing journey.
In the end, we will be grateful for the lessons.

———◆———

3

OCTOBER

As a species, we have forgotten it is essential to spend time with Mother Earth. We must sit with her long enough to feel her power, her strength, her wisdom and her guidance.

———◆———

4

OCTOBER

The worst part about refusing to live a spiritual life
is not the harm that it brings to you, it is the harm
that it brings to those around you.

———◆———

5

OCTOBER

Revealing our sacred stories to our sacred friends
is one of the most intimate things we can do
for our healing and theirs.

———◆———

6

OCTOBER

Look above you and you will see our Father.
Look below you and you will see our Mother.
Look within you and you will see our Creator.

———◆———

7

OCTOBER

Acceptance is a place of love.
Compassion is a place of love.
Patience is a place of love.
Humility is a place of love.
Prayer is a place of love.

———◆———

8

OCTOBER

We are constantly walking three paths simultaneously:
living in fear, walking through fear
and enjoying life after that fear.

———◆———

9
OCTOBER

Honesty is always the right direction.

———◆———

10

OCTOBER

If we do good deeds, Creator will see.
And good things will happen.
We don't need to ask.

———◈———

II

OCTOBER

The sacred balance in our hearts is found when
we equally accept love and offer love.

———◆———

12

OCTOBER

To help someone, we don't need to be
perfect, wealthy, young, old, wise, black,
white, educated or indigenous.
All we have to be is compassionate and available.

———◆———

13

OCTOBER

As parents, we don't want to have to clean up after our child, we teach them to clean up after themselves. Then why are we leaving our children to clean up after us? Why are we leaving them a world where they have to pick up and clean Mother Earth? Who is the child and who is the adult in this situation?

———◈———

14

OCTOBER

Many of us are here because of the prayers of others, particularly those from our enemies. We must always remember to pray for those who will not pray for us. This is the way of the Spirit. If I fail to pray for you, I fail to pray for myself, because we are connected.

———◈———

15

OCTOBER

The emotions we feel are simple directions on where to go. Maybe you're in a good place, therefore keep doing what you are doing. If we feel pain, maybe that tells us we are in a place we don't belong or something needs healing. Pursue what is needed.

———◆———

16

OCTOBER

As you walk with Mother Nature, give her all your
worries. Give her everything that doesn't serve your life.
She has a magical way of turning what no longer serves
life into life again; spiritual manure or ash, both make
great spiritual fertilizer.
Nothing is wasted in her economy.

———◆———

17

OCTOBER

Mother Earth's animals constantly remind us
we don't always need humans
to remind us about our humanity.

———◆———

18

OCTOBER

When we are born, there are sacred instructions laid
out before us that show us how to live in harmony and
balance with each other and the world around us.
They have been here long before humanity.
These sacred agreements found on Mother Earth focus on
keeping the flow and rhythm with each other.

———◈———

19

OCTOBER

Hope begins with what dreams carry and faith finishes,
making the impossible possible.

———◈———

20

OCTOBER

If we are stuck, we can always restart.
If we feel stagnant, we can begin again.
If we feel stale, we can refresh.

———◆———

21

OCTOBER

We are poor in spirit when we don't take time to help those who are poor in spirit.

———◆———

22

OCTOBER

Mother Earth is a sacred place. We must get away from
the colonial narrative that tells us some places are
more important than others. As indigenous people, we
understand it's all sacred.

———◈———

23

OCTOBER

Until we have the courage to face our darkness,
we will always see our darkness in others,
whether it is real or an illusion.

———◆———

24

OCTOBER

Simple lessons in life:
1. Pray often.
2. Listen.
3. Show up.
4. Try your best.
5. Repeat.

———◈———

25

OCTOBER

Truth remembers when lies and illusions
try to convince us otherwise.

26

OCTOBER

If we agree we are spiritual beings having a spiritual experience on our spiritual journey, and our journey consists of traveling from innocence to wisdom, there is no reason to take things personally.

27

OCTOBER

Spiritual healing for emotional/physical/mental sickness:
For the lonely; walk among your relatives, Mother Earth.
For the fearful; pray hard and walk among your relatives,
Mother Earth.
For sickness; walk and pray among your relatives,
Mother Earth.
If you still feel sick, stay longer.

28

OCTOBER

Lessons in life are like arrows in your quiver.
They only work if you use them.

———◈———

29

OCTOBER

The problems in our life are made worse by
thinking about our problems and not focusing and
working toward a solution.

———◈———

30

OCTOBER

One of the biggest spiritual problems in our life
is simply not showing up. Sometimes
our fear paralyzes us. We have to remember
life is a participatory journey.

———◈———

31

OCTOBER

Our life's journey is full and rich when
we keep moving forward while always remembering
where we came from.

———◆———

NOVEMBER

I

NOVEMBER

We change the direction of our life by
changing what we focus and pray on.

———◆———

2

NOVEMBER

We are both caterpillar and butterfly
walking through life.

———◈———

3

NOVEMBER

Awareness of one's own humanity
is humanity's new spiritual frontier.

———◆———

4

NOVEMBER

We must always make an effort
to listen to our ancestors. To create a sacred place
and sit with them,
to ask for guidance and help.
This takes time.
Be patient; the patience you show them
will be offered back to you. The love
you show them will be offered back you.

———◆———

5

NOVEMBER

The same God that made the Earth made you.
The same God that made the Universe made you.
The same God that created Love created you.
The same God that created all life created you.

———◆———

6

NOVEMBER

Compassion is a medicine that teaches us gentleness, the way to the Spirit. It is a powerful message that we send out to the universe.

7

NOVEMBER

When we are standing strong and solid
with our ancestors, our vision will be clear
even if the road isn't straight.

———◆——

8

NOVEMBER

Every season is a sacred circle within a much larger sacred circle. Every part of our life is a sacred circle within a much larger sacred circle. Put together, all these are a much larger sacred circle. Our life is a sacred circle.

———◈———

9

NOVEMBER

The prayers of Mother Earth have always been
for humanity to find its humanity. Love, peace,
balance, and harmony.

———◆———

10

NOVEMBER

A seed can grow silently, but not without help from
Mother Earth, Grandfather Sun, and Grandmother Water.
This a strong and powerful message to humanity.

———◆———

II

NOVEMBER

What gives power to the storms of life is our fear of them.
What the spiritually strong do is ask
for power and direction to get through
and find the lesson.

———◈———

12

NOVEMBER

Fear is our teacher.
Sadness is our teacher.
Happiness is our teacher.
Tears are our teacher.
Humility is our teacher.
Gentleness is our teacher.
Listening is our teacher.

———◆———

13

NOVEMBER

Humanity has created thousands
of languages but it has yet to master one:
the language of the heart.

———◆———

14

NOVEMBER

Just because it feels comfortable
doesn't mean it is in alignment
with what is right or healthy.

———◆———

15

NOVEMBER

There is a sacred circle in all of us where
Mother Earth belongs. Our journey is to find
that place; this is where our peace begins.

———◆———

16

NOVEMBER

If you are behind on your prayers,
today is a great day to catch up.
If you're behind on sharing your love,
today is a great day to catch up.
If you are behind on your dreams,
today is a great day to catch up.
If you are behind on accepting love,
today is a great day to catch up.
If you are behind on telling loved ones you love them,
today is a great day to catch up.
If you're behind on telling yourself you love you,
today is a great day to catch up.
If you are behind on telling Mother Earth you are grateful,
today is a great day to catch up.
If you are behind on honoring your ancestors,
today is a great day to catch up.
If you are behind on your thank you,
today is a great day to catch up.
If you are behind on your gratitude,
today is a great day to catch up.

17

NOVEMBER

When we forget Mother Earth is holy and sacred,
we forget to treat Mother Earth as holy and sacred.

———◈———

18

NOVEMBER

Remember, when we are complaining
about how bad our life is,
someone else is losing theirs.

———◆———

19

NOVEMBER

When we see the heart of the Spirit,
we see the heart of the Spirit
in everything.

———◆———

20

NOVEMBER

Saying "I'm sorry" when wrong is not a weakness.
It doesn't take away from your flame,
it adds to it.

———◆———

21

NOVEMBER

As Indigenous, we believe we are born with a set of
instructions for life; these are ancient agreements of
harmony and balance between humanity and
all life. We must follow these like those who
have come before us, our ancestors. They
understood the instructions have been gifted to us,
and they are to be honored. They will lead us to
a good life. A life of healing in the face of obstacles
and fears. A way of light in the darkness. They
will bring balance in the face of imbalance;
harmony in the face of disharmony.

———◆———

22

NOVEMBER

Every day we must offer ourselves in a good way,
and we will be received in a good way.
We must learn to leave nothing but good prayers
in our wake. We must learn to help in the
healing of others and help love others when they
can't love themselves. These are lessons that
we can give ourselves.

———◆———

23

NOVEMBER

The rivers, forest, mountains and oceans are
all hospitals for the emotionally, physically
and spiritually wounded.

———◆———

24
NOVEMBER

The biggest disease in this world is spiritual poverty,
our lack of awareness and connection to all things,
up to and including ourselves.

25

NOVEMBER

We are blessed to have many mothers, not just our
birth mothers. Each is unique, wonderful and powerful.
Grandmother Moon: the 13 moons each year, 13
grandmothers. Grandmother Ocean:
full of strength and beauty. And of course,
Mother Earth, for she is both
Mother and Grandmother.

———◈———

26

NOVEMBER

The Spirit of life lives in every breath we take.

———◈———

27

NOVEMBER

Let our prayers,
not our opinions, guide us.

———◆———

28

NOVEMBER

Our hope shouldn't depend on circumstances
but on our faith.

———◆———

29

NOVEMBER

Our willingness to surrender to Creator
is one of humanity's most untapped and unused
personal powers.

———◈———

30

NOVEMBER

Are you listening to Mother Earth?
If you're not, why not?
If you are, what is she saying?
What are her dreams?
What are her prayers?

———◆———

DECEMBER

I

DECEMBER

To help change this world, we don't want to fight the old.
We want to begin by simply introducing the new.
We must bring in the Spirit.

———◈———

2

DECEMBER

The hardest part of our spiritual journey
is avoiding it.

———◆———

3

DECEMBER

Our sacred center is that place within that holds the flame of love, compassion, empathy, confidence and faith. It holds the songs and dances of our ancestors. When we guard our sacred center, our sacred center guards us.

———◈———

4

DECEMBER

Humility is one of our most effective
spiritual currencies.

———◆———

5

DECEMBER

Sometimes the best healing we can do for others
is simply plant the seed.

———◆———

6

DECEMBER

Unhealed wounds are untapped wisdom.

———◈———

7

DECEMBER

The "We are love" spiritual mantra is true but it doesn't take away the fact that we are human and in need of healing. To be human means we are flawed. We all have shortcomings and character defects. To be wounded by life, whether it be circumstantially, inadvertently or purposely, means we have a spiritual journey to embark on. And that journey is healing and not faking false positivity. Foregoing this process and switching it with superficial healing to help with childhood trauma is next to spiritually criminal.

We simply have to do the work ourselves.

The only way through is through.

———◆———

8

DECEMBER

Healing is a lifelong process.
It isn't over in a day or as a result
of a healing event.
Time takes time and so does healing.

———◈———

9

DECEMBER

Spiritual freedom begins when we think about
how we can help God instead of
how God can help us.

———◆———

IO

DECEMBER

We don't have to understand Mother Earth to
listen, but we have to listen
to understand Her.

———◈———

II

DECEMBER

If you are looking for a reason to hate
you will always find one.
If you are looking for a reason to love
you will always find one.
If you are looking for a reason to be resentful
you will always find one.
If you are looking for a reason to be compassionate
you will always find one.
If you are looking for a reason to be fearful
you will always find one.
If you are looking for a reason to be grateful
you will always find one.
We will always find what we are looking for.
Question is, what are you looking for?

———◈———

12

DECEMBER

Love, like prayer, means very little without
immediate and appropriate action.

———◆———

13

DECEMBER

The love you have in your God is reflected
in how you treat others who have a different God.

———◆———

14

DECEMBER

Avoiding our spiritual wounds
makes the wounds that much deeper.

———◈———

15

DECEMBER

We all have failed at some point in our lives;
that is human. There is medicine waiting for us
on the other side of failure. Keep trying; when
victory is finally achieved, it gives success a
greater sense of meaning and depth.

———◆———

16

DECEMBER

Our healed darkness is the light
we give to the world.

———◆———

17

DECEMBER

If children aren't educated in the natural rhythms,
harmonies and balance of Mother Earth, then
their education is incomplete.

———◈———

18

DECEMBER

If the faces of our children aren't enough to save
Mother Earth now, then how are we going to save
Mother Earth seven generations from now?

———◆———

19

DECEMBER

Those who are honoring Mother Earth have
spent time listening to her silence, listening to her
wounds, listening to her music, listening to her tears
and listening to her prayers.

———◈———

20

DECEMBER

Eagles and bears don't belong in cages.
But we create our own cages when we live
in fear, resentment, or anger.

———◆———

21

DECEMBER

Life is harder when we refuse
to live a spiritual life.

———◆———

22

DECEMBER

When humanity begins celebrating our diversity,
we will be inadvertently be celebrating our unity.

———◆———

23

DECEMBER

I am made up of all those things I carry with me.
I am made up of all those things I let go.
I am made up of all those things that have healed me.
I am made up of all those things that have wounded me.
I am made up of all those prayers to me.
I am made up of all those prayers I have given.

———◆———

24

DECEMBER

Hidden tears are a form of self-deception,
for they hold an untold story. The process of healing
cannot begin until that story is told.

———◈———

25

DECEMBER

Our investments in Mother Earth should be
trying to save her rather than
taking her resources.

———◆———

26

DECEMBER

The water has memories of Mother Earth and of the
ancestors who came before us.
When we destroy and pollute the water,
we destroy and pollute the memories of
our ancestors and Mother Earth.

———◈———

27

DECEMBER

Listening to our relatives like the trees, the water, the animals, and of course Mother Earth opens the door to bring their strength to bear. Without this relationship, there can be little power, and we will remain weak.

28

DECEMBER

It is hard to handle all the hurts and trauma right now.
That is why God gives us time to heal.
Part of healing is knowing it is a process.
Give time time.

———◆———

29

DECEMBER

Act as if Creator was standing
next to you all the time.

———◆———

30

DECEMBER

It is okay to ask a flower how to bloom.
It is okay to ask a tree how to stay grounded.
It is okay to ask a bird how she learned to fly.
It is okay to ask Mother Earth how to love.

———◈———

31

DECEMBER

When you walk with those with the same mindset,
you find your crowd.
When you walk with the Spirit,
your tribe will find you.
But when you walk with your own heart,
you will find yourself.

———◆———

Daily Medicine

Glossary of Terms

All our relations: a specific Indigenous Spiritual term usually used at the end of our prayer, identifying and in reference to Mother Earth and all who reside on her. All life, plant nations, animals, fish people, winged nations, creepy crawlers, slithery nations, insect nations, fire, water and air.

Ancestor(s): Our past relations, or relatives, those both in physical and spiritual realms.

Ceremony: A particular spiritual event and could also be considered our life's spiritual walk.

Four cardinal directions: East, South, West and North.

Four sacred directions: East, South, West, North, Above, Below and Within.

Great Spirit: A general indigenous term referring to the mighty power of God that flows through all life. The Creator of all life. A life force that is both seen and unseen, male and female.

Hollow Bones: A term coined by our ancestors, about being a conduit for the Great Spirit to work and flow through us becoming a vessel of love, light, healing and life.

Indigenous: Refers to those of ancestral lineage from North, Central and South America.

Love: In spiritual realms, love has nothing to do with physical contact. It means "I want everything good for you but I want nothing from you."

Medicine: In spiritual realms, a thought or idea can be considered medicine. Not just the physical. For example, Love is powerful medicine, it comes in many forms. A thought, a prayer, flowers, a hug. Compassion. Kindness.

Medicine Wheel: Also referred to as the sacred hoop, this is a physical reflection of our spiritual self. It embodies the health and the cycles of life that we live in. This aligns our spiritual life force with those around us, including Mother Earth.

Mother Earth: Our sacred Mother.

Offering(s): Sacred items are given so our prayers will be heard, usually in the form of tobacco or any number of other sacred plant medicines and up to and including ourselves. Always given with sacred intent and purpose.

Prayer: A spiritual request for wisdom, healing, answers and guidance. It is also an opportunity to offer gratitude and thanksgiving.

Red Road: Indigenous spiritual path.

Sacred center: That special and specific place of balance, love and nurturing within us. The God light or the eternal flame within.

Smudge: An act of spiritual cleansing or clearing negative energies, usually by a sacred smoke from sage, cedar, sweet grass or tobacco.

Spiritual Innocence: State of unknowing; pure, like a baby.

Standing Nations: Trees and plants.

Sweat Lodge: A sacred prayer and healing ceremony where we enter into the womb of Mother Earth.

Turtle Island: North America, a name we use as Indigenous referring to the Northern Hemisphere.

Walking in a good way: Our sacred journey through life walking with and for the Great Spirit.

Wound(s): We are speaking in spiritual terms, referring to unhealed emotional hurts including grief, mourning and childhood trauma.

About the Author

Wayne William Snellgrove, a Saulteaux Indian, was born on Fishing Lake First Nation Reserve in Saskatchewan. He is a modern-day genocide survivor of the Canadian government's policy of assimilation known as The 60s Scoop, a two-time USA National swimming champion and a USA Swimming National Team member. He divides his time between the Canadian province of Saskatchewan and the state of Florida in the U.S. with his wife, Charlotte.

CPSIA information can be obtained
at www.ICGtesting.com
Printed in the USA
LVHW011048100720
660315LV00012B/266